BATONS

BATONS

For the
Runners
in the
Race

VALERIE KLERK

WINEPRESS WP PUBLISHING

© 2003 by Valerie Klerk All rights reserved

Printed in the United States of America

Packaged by WinePress Publishing, PO Box 428, Enumclaw, WA 98022. The views expressed or implied in this work do not necessarily reflect those of WinePress Publishing. Ultimate design, content, and editorial accuracy of this work are the responsibilities of the author.

Cover by Ragont Design

No part of this publication may be reproduced, stored in a retrieval system, or transmitted in any way by any means—electronic, mechanical, photocopy, recording, or otherwise—without the prior permission of the copyright holder, except as provided by USA copyright law.

Unless otherwise noted, all Scriptures are taken from the Holy Bible, New International Version, Copyright © 1973, 1978, 1984 by the International Bible Society. Used by permission of Zondervan Publishing House. The "NIV" and "New International Version" trademarks are registered in the United States Patent and Trademark Office by International Bible Society.

ISBN 1-57921-467-3

Library of Congress Catalog Card Number: 2002104101

Therefore, since we are surrounded by such a great cloud of witnesses, let us throw off everything that hinders and the sin that so easily entangles, and let us run with perseverance the race marked out for us. Let us fix our eyes on Jesus, the author and perfecter of our faith.
(Hebrews 12:1,2a)

Preface

Batons for the runners in the race.
    A moment of relief . . .
    A cool splash of refreshing water . . .
    Encouragement to go on . . .
Endurance to know that you're not alone.
    Visions of the finish line . . .
    A helping hand when you fall . . .
Batons filled with words given
    as you press on.
As a soul pants for living waters
    . . . may you be filled.
Words written . . . batons handed to you.
So roll them up and hand them out.
Drop them from a plane . . .
    remember to aim . . .
        for the race.
. . . batons to the runners, may the
    grace of the Lord Jesus Christ
        be with you.

                        Valerie Klerk

CONTENTS

Bend in the River 11
Blueprints 13
Children 15
Cradled in Your Arms 17
Crossroad Departures 19
An Echo of Praise 21
Faith 23
Favor, in Thine Eyes? 25
Fires to Stomp Out 27
A Flower Spent 29
Fragile and Waiting 31
Garden of Life 33
Gates of Heaven 35
A Gift for You! 37
Hall of Flames? 39
Hearts Calloused? 41
Hopeful 43
How Is Your Visual Stimuli Today? 45
It's Been Real 47
A Journey, a Path 49
Justified by One 51
A Life Within 53
Mighty Is Your Strength 55
Morning Song for Thee 57
A Mother's Prayer
   "Take Flight My Children" 59
Mounted and Ready 61
No Competition Just Competing 63

Outcasts? 65
Prayer as Incense 67
A Race to Run 69
Rain 71
Scripture Only 73
Self Has Crept In 75
Shadows 77
Silence 79
Sin, a Worldly Bite 81
Soldiers in Your Army 83
Something to Ponder? 85
Souls to Soar 87
Spectrum, Colors of Life 89
To a Friend 91
A Walk to Please 93
We Shall Meet Again 95
Weep Not for Me 97
Welcome to My Heart 99
When Souls Collide 101
Winds of Mercy 103
Words That Wound 105
Songs
    Have You Ever Seen Me? 107
    Snow Capped Mountains 109

Bend in the River

My soul pants after thee,
    and you fill it with living water.
My feet zealous to run for you,
    and yet you teach me how
    to slow dance.
Embraced with your love,
    the world drifts by . . . as you
    carry me on the river of life.
To the throne we ascend,
    snags lurk beneath, obstacle, and
    trials seek to rip the hull of a soul.
Emotions surge . . . waves to overcome.
Battered lives lay on the banks
    of the world, echo as you pass by.
Selfishness, pity, greed, and lust are
    a few of the screams heard.
Guided by the Holy Spirit alert you
    see the journey unfold.
With the sword of the Spirit held up high,
    and the Kings' armor on you await
    the next bend in the river of life.

This encouraging word is brought to you by

WinePress Publishing from the book,
Batons by **Valerie Klerk**.

To order your copy,
call toll-free 877-421-READ

Blueprints

Life is given "signs posted—under construction"
    steps as nails are heard—our journey.
Virtues as boards used to build.
Elevation—what is to come of life.
Words—the echo of the hearts praise.
A soul—a fortress built to protect humanity
    of the world's injustice.
A will freely given by the master builder.
Have you looked at the plans of life?
Who will you get to build it?
    Yourself? The world?
Empty chambers echo within.
Do you build on the rock?
Does the word of God consume the rooms built
    of self, or things collected from this world?
When the torrent winds of life blows—will you find your
    structure strength from the rock it is built upon?
Do you cry help only when the construction of self
    has come tumbling down?
Does the weariness of this earthly
    body halt construction?
Have you looked at the blueprints . . .
    the Word of God at all?

This encouraging word is brought to you by

WinePress Publishing from the book,
Batons by **Valerie Klerk**.

To order your copy,
call toll-free 877-421-READ

Children

The delight you have given,
    in the children, oh God,
        is beyond measure.
The bounce of laughter as
    they eagerly share.
Their chatter, an overflow
    of their heart.
The sincerity as they explain what
    they are about to accomplish.
To hear the gaiety in their voices,
    as they play.
Reassuring themselves all is okay.
Awe, a gift beyond measure.
To gaze at their smile . . .
    a cup filled . . . bursting out
    with the life you have given.
A simple touch . . . a gesture of love.
A silent moment of a soul.
Thank you for the children, oh Lord.

This encouraging word is brought to you by

WinePress Publishing from the book,
Batons by **Valerie Klerk**.

To order your copy,
call toll-free 877-421-READ

Cradled in Your Arms

Gazing upon the vastness of the stars
    scattered in the heavens.
Breathless as one ponders the magnitude
    of an awesome God.
Time ticks away . . . an infant in wisdom
    and life compared to eternity.
A flicker of light glistens, a reflection of a soul
    as your word echoes within.
Held in the arms of a merciful God.
    In our frail weakness your strength abounds.
Hearing our cries . . . your compassion flows.
And in the quiet moments you whisper so.
Tugging our hearts softly closer to thee.
An eternal embrace what joy flows.
When a world runs rampant and
    we feel all alone . . . trusting your promise
    we know you'll never leave us or forsake us . . .
We are just cradled in your arms.

This encouraging word is brought to you by

WinePress Publishing from the book,
Batons by **Valerie Klerk**.

To order your copy,
call toll-free 877-421-READ

Crossroad Departures

On the crossroads we have met,
    strangers walking a narrow path.
We never know whom we will meet on
    His path, or the lives we touch.
Our time has been brief and your kindness
    has touched my life.
Even though you'll only be a short distance
    away, our daily path will cease.
Keep the faith, and when you stumble . . .
    keep the light of His Word close so
    you may walk again.
Remember to seek refuge in the time
    of the storm. If you forget how to find
    the shelter, see map Matthew 6:33 & 7:7.
When the sharks are in a feeding frenzy,
    keep your focus on Jesus and you'll
    walk away on water.
Jesus had no place to rest his head, if
    you have more . . . you're blessed!
Crossroad departures . . . so sad.
May the riches of God's grace that he
    lavished on us with all wisdom
    and understanding light your path.

This encouraging word is brought to you by

WinePress Publishing from the book,
Batons by **Valerie Klerk**.

To order your copy,
call toll-free 877-421-READ

An Echo of Praise

Hear the cry of praise,
    echoing from your remnant today.
Jesus Christ the Son of God
    for an eternity be praised.
Mercy, oh Lord, on a soul
    as they seek your face.
Grip a heart in the youth of a life,
    keeping them on your straight way.
Show us our hidden sins,
    so rigid within.
A soul molded in your mercy
    dances singing your praise
    as we labor through today.
Break the silence of your army,
    that your praise may be heard
    throughout the land.
Vibrating the very souls of man.
As we seek you early in the day,
    lead us in your way.
As a voice in the wilderness making
    straight the way, in this world
    we live in today.
A roar as a mighty wave, your army
    marches a dance of praise.
Come, Lord Jesus we pray, as we
    echo your praise.
Omnipotent, sovereign, and merciful
almighty God are your ways.

This encouraging word is brought to you by

WinePress Publishing from the book,
Batons by **Valerie Klerk**.

To order your copy,
call toll-free 877-421-READ

Faith

Where shall my steps lead, oh Lord.
Will you carry me, or will I walk
    on the strength you give.
The world crushes the hope, darkens
    the vision enveloped in self.
Faith a window of hope,
    visions of your promises . . .
    Never to leave us . . .
A dance of praise . . . simple
    chores of the day fold.
A heart grateful of the lessons
    learned, forever to hold.
Troubles befall us, and a
    heart bellows its wants.
Forgetting where they have come
    from or where they are going.
Free falling in a world of hopelessness.
Faith a window of hope,
    visions of your promises . . .
    Never to forsake us . . .
Faith . . . God is with us!

This encouraging word is brought to you by

WinePress Publishing from the book,
***Batons* by Valerie Klerk.**

To order your copy,
call toll-free 877-421-READ

Favor, in Thine Eyes?

Where shall I go today,
    What will my steps say?
A life filled with your Word,
    beats within a heart this day.
Your Son Jesus lights my way.
Carried on the winds of the
    Holy Spirit.
A world full of sin, berates one
    with a harshness of a violent wind.
But in the stillness of a soul, will it
    be pages of your Word that unfold?
Steps of a soul, will they find favor
    in thine eyes?
In obedience we patiently await
    your return.
Favor found in the arms of a
    sovereign God.
A life blessed for our trust is in thee.
Let the magnitude of your Word be
    heard in our steps today.
Gentleness, love, patience,
    perseverance and self control.
Steps of a soul . . .
    as the pages of life unfold.
Let your glory illuminate a soul that
    has given you full control.

Merciful in all your ways . . .
    as this world tries to blow us away.
Favor from an almighty God . . .
    steps of a soul firmly planted
    in His way.

This encouraging word is brought to you by

WinePress Publishing from the book,
Batons by **Valerie Klerk**.

To order your copy,
call toll-free 877-421-READ

Fires to Stomp Out

When the world enrages around you
    like flames of a fire.
Living water flows from the throne
    of God. Heaven sent and refreshes
    the soul.
Shall we blaze the fires until we are
    at our wits end?
Storms to engulf our faith.
How many times have we all stood
    at this place?
Hold fast to the measure of faith
    given by an omnipotent God.
His Word smolders the flames of
    this world.
A new day brings flowers in a
    charred world.

This encouraging word is brought to you by

WinePress Publishing from the book,
Batons by **Valerie Klerk**.

To order your copy,
call toll-free 877-421-READ

A Flower Spent

To my friend in Christ.
Whatever betides you, remember Jesus is beside you
    as long as you stay in His narrow way.
Sorrow for the moment of our departing.
But I have to lift my praise to Him who sits on the throne
    and to the Lamb, that has given us grace along our way.

A life hidden in Christ. Cherished moments together . . .
    a season spent, flowers in full bloom.
Tears within . . . from the weeds He has pulled.
    A life in His garden, you know how it has been.
Now, carried by His winds . . . to plant seeds, and water
    for His garden spans out wide. To see the miracle
    of His growth . . . a moment in time, a season spent.
Be alert my friend or the weeds will creep in.
    Faithfully tend to the ones He sends.

Let your conversation be always full of grace,
    seasoned with salt, the flavor of eternal life.
Gird your mind to protect what He has given thine.
Be diligent in His Word, keep busy and live a quiet life.
Teach your children while they're young . . . God's way, and
    when they're old they will not depart to the world's way.
Pray without ceasing, for this is a life within.
Quietly in the closet of your heart,
    you commune with the almighty God.

His Holy Spirit is like the wind; you don't know where it comes
from or where it is going, but this you can trust.
He will comfort you in time of need, convict you if you fall.
Teach and guide you in God's truth for all.
Check the focus of your soul, is it Jesus you behold?
The future is yet to come, but it is in the today that we touch
eternity. We must be about our Father's business.

Weak and weary, don't let Satan in with his words that deceive
trying to carry you in the world's wind.
Hold fast when your faith is tried, put on the whole armor of God.
The helmet of salvation . . . knowing that you are saved.
His breastplate of righteous . . . right standing in His sight.
With the belt of truth and with your feet fitted with the
readiness that comes from the gospel of peace . . .
to walk the steps that Christ has been.
Take up the shield of faith . . .
extinguished the flaming arrows of the evil one.
With the sword of the spirit . . . His Word.
Fight the battle . . . Keep the faith . . .
just a flower in His garden, spent.
Until another bloom, my friend . . .

This encouraging word is brought to you by

WinePress Publishing from the book,
Batons by **Valerie Klerk**.

To order your copy,
call toll-free 877-421-READ

Fragile and Waiting

To bask in light of your Son,
    to lay a life at His feet.
Within the quietness of a soul He hears a
    heart beat, longing to be complete.
Illness befalls us and we know not why . . .
With a new body we shall meet Him in the sky.
To heaven through the blue sky our
    praises meet Him on high.
Riddled with affliction from living in a world of sin,
    this old body has been cleansed from within.
Gentleness as your hand of mercy untangles
    the web the world weaves.
With obedience we shall be led,
    by the Master's hand.
Follow we must . . .
    listening for your every command.
A soul dances from a fragile body.
Sovereign in all your ways,
    we lift our praise.
To our King, to our Lord, Jesus your Son.
Filled with your love and overflowing . . .
    waiting for His return.

This encouraging word is brought to you by

WinePress Publishing from the book,
Batons by **Valerie Klerk**.

To order your copy,
call toll-free 877-421-READ

Garden of Life

Do we sow kindness? Do we sow love?
Have we allowed God to break our fallow ground.
Has our life been tilled . . . pliable . . . ready to use.
Have our steps been as graceful as a flower pedal.
In the solitude of unspoken beauty of an iris
    does our soul flourish?
As you garden, my friend, you come to realize
    how the master gardener tends to our soul.
We look hard for the labor of our hand,
    but realize without God nothing grows.
Time fades as the years drift by, and we
    never know who God may send our way.
Hold fast to His Word,
    let His Son shine bright on you.
Remember we're just flowers in His garden.
Just something to ponder, as your life
    awaits for another season in His garden.

This encouraging word is brought to you by

WinePress Publishing from the book,
Batons by **Valerie Klerk**.

To order your copy,
call toll-free 877-421-READ

Gates of Heaven

Heavens gates open wide,
    stretching out across the hillside.
A city beaming with the glory of God.
Angels flying high,
    meeting us in the sky.
With His arms out stretched wide
    Jesus gazes over the countryside.
"Welcome ye blessed of my Father"
His words echo . . .
    vibrating the very soul of man.
Your life flashes before you,
    and it was like you heard Him say.
Tired and weary from the cares of this world,
    you walked on.
Embraced with love,
    that came from above.
Shining stars in a dark sinful world.
Now through grace, come look at this place.
With heaven's gates opened wide,
    you go inside.
Ah, an eternity so divine.

This encouraging word is brought to you by

WinePress Publishing from the book,
Batons by **Valerie Klerk**.

To order your copy,
call toll-free 877-421-READ

A Gift for You!

A life, a gift from God
How awesome to hold a new life.
To cradle an infant in your arms,
    to caress the steps they may take
        with the love of Jesus.
The magnitude of the sovereign Triune God
    to have bestowed a gift so wonderful.
How your heart leaps within at first sight,
    tiny fingers so softly held at birth.
Gently reassuring them of your presence,
    as you stroke their brow.

Oh Lord God, thank you for this gift.
There's so much to learn, and so much beauty
    in this world that God has made, my little one.
With kindness, patience and love I shall travel
    with thee only a short time.
Before I know it, you will be grown,
    taking flight to a nest of your own.
But for now Jesus has given you to me,
    and through His strength we'll learn to
    dance a life of praise to His glory.

Spring we'll learn of the new life He has
    given us through His own Son.
Summer we'll learn through the heat of a trial,
    that He overcame a trial in a desert.

Fall we'll learn how colorful life is as we watch
    and play in the leaves He made be.
Winter we'll learn the importance of solitude,
    to be still and listen for His voice.
Softly spoken like footsteps in a powdery snow,
His voice . . . as footsteps to guide you
    through life, will echo from His Word.
My little one, so much awaits you.

This encouraging word is brought to you by

WinePress Publishing from the book,
Batons by **Valerie Klerk**.

To order your copy,
call toll-free 877-421-READ

Hall of Flames?

Fog as a blanket covers the world today.
People seeking self are led astray.
Scales as a mist obstruct the eyes,
    of a soul.
The vivid colors of sin, a fog a lost soul
    wanders in.
Blinded and led astray by sin,
    eternal damnation is the prize to win.
A palette of colors, discord, greed, lust,
    witchcraft, envy, jealousy, sexual immorality,
    selfish ambitions, and the like.
A life . . . a canvas the world paints with
    the brush of self, vivid colors of sin.
The devil cheers within . . . a masterpiece the
    world has given me, for my gallery.
Prepared by the almighty God you'll see.
Eternal fire for me and my angels . . .
    eternal flames will be our fame.
Agony, pain and despair will be
    the artist there.
In God's love He has given the world His Son
    and a choice to see . . .
    if we only believe in Jesus . . .
    eternal life we'll see.
A life painted with His Holy Spirit, love, joy,
    peace, patience, kindness, goodness,

faithfulness, gentleness and self-control,
colors of eternal life you see.
The choice is yours . . . will you believe?
Or will your life be hung in the Hall of Flames?

This encouraging word is brought to you by

WinePress Publishing from the book,
Batons by **Valerie Klerk**.

To order your copy,
call toll-free 877-421-READ

Hearts Calloused?

Hardness of heart . . . jealousy crept in
Selfishness sparked by envy
Evil seeks to devour like a roaring lion
Where is the heart of the giver,
Where has the kindness gone,
Where are the words of praise
    almighty God?

Mercy on one that falls short.
From the heart of the innocence
    your giving heart springs forth.

Untarnished love—pure and overflowing.
    Bubbling over with praise
      from the hearts of babes.

This encouraging word is brought to you by

WinePress Publishing from the book,
Batons by **Valerie Klerk**.

To order your copy,
call toll-free 877-421-READ

Hopeful

My friend, to find the words printed
    on a card to share what flows from
    this heart seems hopeless.
God will provide . . . to trust in Him.

The world hears cancer and hope
    free falls in a dark abyss.
God will provide . . . to trust in Him.

Words a palette of comfort to
    embellished on our friends.
God will provide . . . to trust in Him.

This life on earth is just a breath
    of our eternal life to come.
God will provide . . . to trust in Him.

Illnesses may slay this fleshly body,
    yet I will trust in God.
Sovereign and merciful are His ways.
To create or restore man has always
    been in His hands.
A life cradled in the arms of a God of hope.
In a world filled with hopelessness we
    serve a God of hope.
May His peace be with you, my friend.

This encouraging word is brought to you by

WinePress Publishing from the book,
Batons by **Valerie Klerk**.

To order your copy,
call toll-free 877-421-READ

How Is Your Visual Stimuli Today?

Oh optic nerve,
Numb from the world,
The intense light shines upon you.
Will you be found faultless,
    free of disease.
Will the brilliance of the light
    illuminate as a rainbow when
    shrouded by darkness.
Reflection of this world you do see,
    but how about the reflection of a soul?
Grace given by the Master who looks in,
"The light of the world beams on you today."
How will the Great Physician find
    your optic nerve today?
Grace . . . unmerited favor . . . awe.
What a healing touch to be seen
    and found unblemished.
Don't wander aimlessly through life,
    ask the Master Physician to
    shine His light on your optic nerve today.
The optic nerve through a patient's eyes.

This encouraging word is brought to you by

WinePress Publishing from the book,
Batons by **Valerie Klerk**.

To order your copy,
call toll-free 877-421-READ

It's Been Real

The phone rings, breakfast is burning.
Your mate yells . . . Where are my shoes?
A news flash . . . Severe storm watch today.
The children pull for your attention.
Your heart races.. It's almost time to leave.
Raincoats everyone, you announce.
Out of the corner of vision you see,
    the dog chewing on your shoes.
The door bell rings, a salesman.
No thank you, not today as the door closes.
Frantically you look at the time.
You start to change, the clothes you have laid
    out nice and neatly the night before
    lay wrinkled on the floor.
The children fuss over which raincoat to wear.
The phone rings again, I need a jump my car
    won't start, states your neighbor.
I'll be over in a few minutes, as you hang up the phone.
Your children and mate stand at the door
    awaiting your presence.
As you grab your raincoat you head to the door.
Your family quietly stands in a moment of silence.
As each one gives thanks to God for the day that
    awaits them, and ask Him to be with them.
The lightning thunders, the rain pours.
As you snug up the children's raincoats, you open
    the door ready for the day.

The reality of your life . . .
    Jesus leads you and your family's way.
Instantly the Son breaks the sky, the storm is no more.
You hear a trumpet, a shout, and everyone beholds
    the Son of God.
It's been real, this reality of life.

This encouraging word is brought to you by

WinePress Publishing from the book,
Batons by **Valerie Klerk**.

To order your copy,
call toll-free 877-421-READ

A Journey, a Path

The gaiety of the voices, as they seek you
    . . . echo with excitement.
Eagerly they await,
    . . . the thrill of life.
Adventurously they endeavor
    . . . the trail you have blazed.
A journey, a path to be walked on many times.
Their actions speak with visions
    . . . of their first love.
Tears fall for the lost ones,
    when they're called home.
Hearts saddened, when others
    seek another path.
Not wanting to follow your command.
Self entices, wondering after wants.
Bathe in your love, refuge under the wings
    of your mercy, we sequester ourselves.
In the quietness of the night
    . . . you hear our cries.
The fears that grip our souls, the darkness
    of the world we behold.
The life light of your Word
    illuminates our path, Jesus your Son.
The sadness stretches across the world
    for those who have rejected Him.
Comforted by your Holy Spirit we await your return.

This encouraging word is brought to you by

WinePress Publishing from the book,
Batons by **Valerie Klerk**.

To order your copy,
call toll-free 877-421-READ

Justified by One

The wind of heaven blows across your soul,
    embraced with a conviction of guilt.
Life passes before your eyes,
    gripped with the vision of purity.
You stand in awe . . . could this be my life?
Wind of heaven I searched and could not
    find where you have come from
    or where you're going.
A lamp on a narrow path has been laid before me.
    Travel I must, this road.
The journey a moment in time.
Held up high the lamp illuminates the path,
    words are seen . . . you recognize them.
"For God so loved the world . . ."
    you noticed diamonds lay all on the path.
A gentle breeze is heard, tears of repentance,
    and you question the diamonds no longer.
Distant thunder echoes as you approach
    the end of the path.
Enveloped with light you now stand before
    the throne of God.
Judgment day . . . Father, Jesus said, as He looked
    at me. Justified by my blood, the narrow path
    was traveled holding on to me.
You stand in awe . . . could this be my life.

This encouraging word is brought to you by

WinePress Publishing from the book,
Batons by **Valerie Klerk**.

To order your copy,
call toll-free 877-421-READ

A Life Within

To wield a page that would not bend,
    His Word our sword has always been.
Coldness of the world tries to envelop,
    seeking to devour.
With phantom calls of desire, it plagues
    one with self.
Greed, lust and covetousness all become
    a must.
Accosted by His Word, His sword
    a page that would not bend.
A heart dances from within,
    with the fluttering of praise.
To Jesus Christ my Lord and Savior,
    for on the cross He was raised.
Shrouded in the cold darkness of this world
    for three days, His light was still a blaze.
Death had no reign, on your life
    forever to reign.
With your arms stretched out wide,
    you so willingly died.
Let us not hide,
    your Word that dwells within.
A soul willing to bend,
    to your Word that has always been.

This encouraging word is brought to you by

WinePress Publishing from the book,
Batons by **Valerie Klerk**.

To order your copy,
call toll-free 877-421-READ

Mighty Is Your Strength

From heaven you shout and earth shakes.
    Mighty is your strength.
Merciful in your ways, refuge in the time of storm.
    Mighty is your strength.
A healing touch of the Masters hand, and healing virtue flows.
    Mighty is your strength.
The flesh inflicted with the agony of a worldly sting . . . sin.
    Mighty is your strength.
Illness invade our bodies, death eminent.
    Mighty is your strength.
Yet, you gave Hezekiah fifteen more years.
    Mighty is your strength.
Shrouded in worldly coldness . . . a new body you will restore.
    Mighty is your strength.
For an eternity we shall sing your praise, oh Lord Jesus.
    Mighty is your strength.

This encouraging word is brought to you by

WinePress Publishing from the book,
Batons by **Valerie Klerk**.

To order your copy,
call toll-free 877-421-READ

Morning Song for Thee

Do you hear an ocean breeze
    under the autumn leaves.
Can you see the colors sparkle
    on the crystal sea.
A dance with thee, in the early
    morning light.
A gentle breeze has given flight.
Soaring on the highest thermal,
    the waves of life crash below.
Jesus this praise is for
    your delight . . . my flight.
From glory to glory you lead
    teaching me along my way.
Stories of old told, unfold from
    a heart of a child.
Echoes of your Word . . .
    strength that lights the way.
A journey, this flight of life.
May the winds of your Holy Spirit
    guide me to you, oh merciful God.
From an ocean breeze to autumn leaves
    my heart sings to thee.

This encouraging word is brought to you by

WinePress Publishing from the book,
Batons by **Valerie Klerk**.

To order your copy,
call toll-free 877-421-READ

A Mother's Prayer
"Take Flight My Children"

Gripped with a mother's passion, freely released
    to soar to the throne of God.
Take hold my children she cries,
    to the horns of the altar of God.
    Place your lives in the mercy seat.
Lay prostrate as God lavishes the riches of
    His merciful grace upon you.
In humility be thankful for the demonstration
of His merciful power he bestows upon you!
    Keep the door of your heart open . . .
    that His praises may be heard.
The silence of your heart may it be captivated with
    the awesomeness of the Triune God you serve.
Walk in His truth. Let the vibration of His gentleness
    be evident to all.
Gripped with His compassion . . . let forgiveness flow.
Hear the echoes of a mothers' passion . . .
    Keep the faith. Keep the fight.
May the grace of our Lord Jesus Christ be
    with you on your life journey.
Fly my children on the wings of His grace!

This encouraging word is brought to you by

WinePress Publishing from the book,
Batons by **Valerie Klerk**.

To order your copy,
call toll-free 877-421-READ

Mounted and Ready

Breathe on us Lord Jesus
    that life may be given.
Your word sinew to the
    bones of the soul.
A vast army, a remnant
    raised for a king.
Awaiting His return, as the hoof
    beats are heard all over
    this land.
"Come ride with me,"
His voice echoes through the
    mountain tops and valleys
    of the soul.
"Come," he calleth.
Has the clamor of the world's dry bones
    deafened you with its demands?
How many times will God draw
    and heated by your desires, shrivel.
Captivated by the awesomeness of a gentle,
    merciful grip of a mighty God.
Strengthen through Christ, our life's breath
    to a soul, mounted ready.
Quiet moments in the stillness of the soul's heart,
    with the world raging a flood of blood
    of countless murdered souls . . .
Flows to the horse's bridle height.
We await your command . . .
Hear the echoes of the souls manifested,
    "Come quickly Lord Jesus."

This encouraging word is brought to you by

WinePress Publishing from the book,
Batons by **Valerie Klerk**.

To order your copy,
call toll-free 877-421-READ

No Competition Just Competing

Competition drives one to achieve,
    the prize . . . prosperity to the winner.
A measure, a legend for self worth.
To the loser . . . their inability to
    measure up to their peers.
Monetary prizes . . . worldly rewards.
To the winner . . . recognition of success.
To the loser . . . recognition of failure.
Worldly competition judges one
    by one's material possession.
We are to compete in a race though.
The race is the life we live on earth
    in Christ Jesus.
Agape drives one to achieve.
The prize . . . eternal life just to finish.
Competition is replaced by encouragement.
Encouragement to up lift other runners . . .
Success measured by the heart . . .
    not performance.
No competition, just competing.

This encouraging word is brought to you by

WinePress Publishing from the book,
Batons by **Valerie Klerk**.

To order your copy,
call toll-free 877-421-READ

Outcasts?

Are we outcasts in your family, oh Lord?
Unable to put a man-made label on our faith,
 a religious title.
To be recognized with a group, sealed with
 their approval, cradled in their friendship.
As in the days of Elijah you have a remnant,
 and they sing your praise.
Some with and without labels on their faith.
Sealed with your Holy Spirit, bathed with
 your grace . . .
Recognized by the fruit they bare . . .
Cradled in your friendship they go about
 your business.
Parched and wandering in a wilderness
 of religion.
We search for the rock where the living
 waters flow.
We await our promise land, a new heaven,
 a new earth.
Search our hearts and purge our hidden sins.
Outcasts from man-made religions,
 but part of your family, the remnant.
That eagerly seek your Son,
 Jesus and His return.

This encouraging word is brought to you by

WinePress Publishing from the book,
***Batons* by Valerie Klerk**.

To order your copy,
call toll-free 877-421-READ

Prayer as Incense

Rustle of the leaves, a cool crisp morning breeze.
Prayers as incense to heaven they ascend.
Before your throne . . .
    a sweet savor of your saints unfold.
Colors of our lives as leaves in autumn fall.
Time drifts by, the seasons of life unfold,
    not knowing what is yet to behold.
Awesome in your mercy, sovereign in all
    your ways, to you I shall call.
The dew from heaven descend on a
    delicate flower pedal.
Intricately fashioned by your almighty hand,
    glistens with light you have given.
Let a life be as such, oh Lord God.
Let your living water flow through the veins
    of a soul.
Holy Spirit as the dew from heaven
    descend upon me.
Son of God, Jesus my Lord . . . shine brightly
    that this life may glisten with your light.
May your Holy Spirit, as a gentle breeze rustle
    the leaves of a soul as praise to thee.
Heard throughout this earth you made be.
Intricately fashioned by the life of your Son.
Refuge to warm a soul . . .
    from the world's cold breeze.
A prayer as incense for thee.

This encouraging word is brought to you by

WinePress Publishing from the book,
Batons by **Valerie Klerk**.

To order your copy,
call toll-free 877-421-READ

A Race to Run

To run a race, a quest for an eternity.
To be pressed from all sides and
    yet, to just abide.
Obstacles of this world befall us,
    overcomers running on a narrow path.
The course blazed by His Son long ago, sent to us
    as a gift by a merciful God, you know.
To believe in His Son, Jesus—the rules for this race.

The distant cries beckon our attention,
    trusting in the rock foundation,
    we fall short only to be justified.
Illusions as a roaring lion seeks to devour
    and a wind as a whisper is heard, "Be still."
Confusion, crime, gossip, and jealousy are
    wounds to a runner, but to run in harmony
    is to be healed by His stripes.

Treacherous at times and this earthly body grows
    faint until you wait upon the Lord
    and strength is renewed.
To the valleys from the mountain peaks and through
    the meadows to the rushing rivers or to a gentle
    stream this narrow road we journey on.

Pace yourself with faith, goodness, knowledge, self-control,
perseverance, godliness, brotherly kindness
and love that your steps may be sure.
And remember it is His grace—unmerited favor
that entered us in this race.

This encouraging word is brought to you by

WinePress Publishing from the book,
Batons by **Valerie Klerk**.

To order your copy,
call toll-free 877-421-READ

Rain

Distant thunder echoes from heaven,
    a soul knelt before thy throne.
Forgive us our sins, replenish our soul
    with your life giving water.
Deliver us from the storms of this world.
Carry us on the wind of heaven, from
    glory to glory, as you nourish our soul.
Echoes from your throne thunders.
Omnipotent . . . a soul stands in awe.
Sovereign . . . to be still and know you are God.
Merciful . . . tears of repentance flow.
My Son . . . a gift received.
Jesus, hear a dance of praise as rain drops
    from a thankful soul.
As the roar of a gentle rain, may your
Word forever resound in this soul.

This encouraging word is brought to you by

WinePress Publishing from the book,
Batons by **Valerie Klerk**.

To order your copy,
call toll-free 877-421-READ

Scripture Only

A heart crushed by the ignorance of humanity.
Led blindly into the gates to hell.
Penance they diligently paid
    unknowingly with their soul.
Striving to obtain a falsehood of the
    Antichrist this world demands.
To feel confident and reassured by man.
Aimlessly they wander lost in
    an abyss of sin.
Seeking a righteousness sanctioned by man.
Gripped by compassion by a merciful God.
Tears of repentance flow to be loved so much,
    to have a glimpse of His Son.
To be drawn closer by the almighty God.
Humbled to be loved so much that He
    gave His only begotten Son.
The redeemer of mankind Jesus of Nazareth.
Seek first His kingdom and His righteousness.
You alone, oh God, are to be feared.
Omnipotent in all your ways,
    to have touched a heart this way.

This encouraging word is brought to you by

WinePress Publishing from the book,
Batons by **Valerie Klerk**.

To order your copy,
call toll-free 877-421-READ

Self Has Crept In

Oh Lord Jesus your wisdom is infinite,
    and our minds are finite.
The morning birds singing their melody,
    and a soul only squawks its wants.
Crying as a baby not knowing where
    misery has crept in.
Self has germinated misery, a fungus
    to grow in the darkness of despair.
Shine your light, oh Lord Jesus!
    That the growth of a soul
    may rid itself of self!
Let your cleansing blood
    wash away the sin,
Holy Spirit fall upon this soul as a dove;
    guide, lead, comfort and convict, that
    the path taken will be a narrow way
    that leads to the throne of God.
Night has fallen once again,
    to find a soul still on its knees.
Just a touch from the hem of your garment
    and healing virtue flows.
Your mercy endureth forever!
May a soul soar to the heights of heaven
    singing your praise, as rest is given
    under the shelter of your wings.
Good night until another morning light.

This encouraging word is brought to you by

WinePress Publishing from the book,
Batons by **Valerie Klerk**.

To order your copy,
call toll-free 877-421-READ

Shadows

Are we looking through
    a looking glass?
Shadows of a home,
    hanging on the shoulders of
    a frail and fragile world.
When the light of God's glory
    shines . . . steps as images
    of your life unfold.
A world that eclipses your soul . . .
    shadows are lost.
Shadows . . . illnesses that befalls us,
    sin that grips, and trials to overcome.
To walk without a shadow is to walk
    without light.
To grope in an abyss of darkness or
    to see the glory of your light.
Shine brightly Lord Jesus that the
    shadows may not overcome us.

This encouraging word is brought to you by

WinePress Publishing from the book,
***Batons* by Valerie Klerk**.

To order your copy,
call toll-free 877-421-READ

Silence

The vacuum of silence,
    echoes within one's heart.
Vapors of prayer are seen through
    the soul's window.
In our silence God judges.
The distant thunder from a heart,
    beats for thee, oh God.
With a world full of noise that
    fights for your attention.
Demands of the day resound.
The silence pulls you away,
    drifting to the magnitude
    of the God you serve.

This encouraging word is brought to you by

WinePress Publishing from the book,
***Batons* by Valerie Klerk**.

To order your copy,
call toll-free 877-421-READ

Sin, a Worldly Bite

The world's bite is the most
    deadly to the soul of man.
Producing eternal damnation
    throughout this land.
Evil penetrating with its poison,
    paralyzing the minds of man.
No longer working for God
    with their hands.
The blood of Jesus protects us from
    this bite, giving us eternal life.
Repent and be washed from
    the world's bite.
And God's Holy Spirit will be given flight
    sent to us in Jesus' name.
A light to guide us in His truth, teaching us
    how to avoid the world's bite.
Convicting us of the poison
    that is still within.
That one day we may be given flight
    to meet Jesus when he comes as
    a thief in the night.

This encouraging word is brought to you by

WinePress Publishing from the book,
Batons by **Valerie Klerk**.

To order your copy,
call toll-free 877-421-READ

Soldiers in Your Army

March we may, step-by-step
 onward pressing forward.
A dance of praise, a victory cry!
Awe! Jesus Christ our Lord.
A dance of laughter for the joy
 that overflows.
A cry is heard, "It is finished!"
 and the battle is won.
Echoes throughout Eternity.
 King of kings,
 Lord of lords.
We ride triumphant with our
 swords held up high.
Jesus Christ has blazed our way.
 Soldiers marching His way.
Vibrating the land with the magnitude
 of our praise for thee.
Dressed and ready for battle,
 we await your return . . .
 our next command.

This encouraging word is brought to you by

WinePress Publishing from the book,
Batons by **Valerie Klerk**.

To order your copy,
call toll-free 877-421-READ

Something to Ponder?

Do you want to hear of heart aches?
I'll tell you of a man whose friend was beheaded,
then served 5000 men and their families.

Do you want to hear of rejection?
How about a Son at his death,
his Father could not look upon Him.

Do you want to hear of hardship?
Birds have nests, Foxes have holes,
but this man has no place to lay His head.

Do you want to hear of loneliness?
Late one night at a point of despair
in a garden, you can hear a single cry,
"Father," as He prayed.

How does the world find you? Do you share your
secret joys? Do you cry yourself to sleep? Do you
find yourself walking in the darkness? Have you seen the light?
If not, you're only a heartbeat away from eternity.

Let me tell you about compassion.
Gripped with the pain inflicted by His accuser . . .
a prayer was offered up for them, forgiveness, as they
crucify Him.

Let me tell you about giving.
Think about the most terrible person you have
ever known or read of. Would you lay down your life
for them? He did.

Let me tell you about grace.
Unmerited favor, to be justified, presented unblemished
before a holy God. Price paid for sin. Adoption paperwork.
A gift given by the almighty God. An unbreachable
communion with a sovereign God.

Why do we ponder such thoughts? Do we search for His footsteps?
Has the focus been on our life and the trials that are inflicted upon us
by this world? When you focus on Jesus Christ and what the
world inflicted upon him your troubles seem so small. When
life seems to get you down . . . ponder His footsteps . . .
so easily seen in the gospel.

This encouraging word is brought to you by

WinePress Publishing from the book,
Batons by **Valerie Klerk**.

To order your copy,
call toll-free 877-421-READ

Souls to Soar

A soul ripped from a heart soars
    to the cross—and God beholds,
    a servant dancing before His throne.
Cleansed with the blood of His Son,
    unblemished we stand before the
    mighty strength of an awesome God.
On our knees we fall in gratitude
    for the love He has shown us.
Fly we must . . . on the golden clouds
    of His blessing . . . our trust in Him alone.
With a mighty stroke of His hand He
    sifts the graves as sand.
Gathering the treasured souls of
    saints of old.
Fly we must . . . souls to soar
    on the winds of His Holy Spirit
    praises are heard.
Refreshed as we drink from His living word.
Fly we must . . . souls to soar
    mighty in His strength!
Fly we must . . .

This encouraging word is brought to you by

WinePress Publishing from the book,
Batons by **Valerie Klerk**.

To order your copy,
call toll-free 877-421-READ

Spectrum, Colors of Life

Spectrum of your Word, colors of life as
    your light illuminates within a heart.
Search us, oh God, let your merciful grace
    flow through the veins of a soul
        . . . giving eternal life.
Filled with thanksgiving for your love
    shown to man.
For giving your Son, and for His walk
    as a man.
Spectrum of life, colors of grace, reflected
    by the love you almighty God had for
    this world.
The echo of your praise bounces off
    this heart raised.
To the heavens may it soar for your glory
    . . . my Lord.
Bent to repentance this prism heart,
    by the light of your Son . . .
Spectrum of your Word, colors of eternal life.

This encouraging word is brought to you by

WinePress Publishing from the book,
Batons by **Valerie Klerk**.

To order your copy,
call toll-free 877-421-READ

To a Friend

Time as seasons of our lives come and go,
    soon to be no more.
Spent as faded flowers, but today
    we live in full bloom.
The fragrance of our life could be as a rose,
    permeating the air to all that pass our way.
This will be determined by what flows into
    the soul of man.
Take hold my friend . . . Each moment that the
    almighty Triune God has blessed us with.
Let it be the living water given by Christ
    that fills your life.
Cherish the moments with the gift God has
    given you, your children.
Seek for the knowledge as gold, that you are
    to teach them.
Embrace those that Christ sends your way.
And if they be as a thorn,
    wear them as Christ did.
With compassion from your soul as a
    soft gentle touch of a rose petal.
Grace be with you . . . always remember you're held
    in the arms of a merciful God.

This encouraging word is brought to you by

WinePress Publishing from the book,
Batons by **Valerie Klerk**.

To order your copy,
call toll-free 877-421-READ

A Walk to Please

Oh Lord not knowing what the
    future beholds.
We lay our lives in the arms of
    a merciful God to hold.
Sovereign in all your ways,
    you shall direct our way.
A gentle breeze flows through the leaves,
    we are as the trees.
Standing still on your Word,
    hoping to please.
As the rustle of the leaves,
    we sing our praise to thee.
Branches of life, travel so many ways,
    I will direct your steps, I heard Him say.
A world full of decisions,
    a journey full of incision.
Lead us to walk with your peace.
Grip our hearts before we start,
    on a path that will sadden our hearts.
Tears from the cuts of this world,
    healed by your stripes . . .
    we await another world.
Your Son Jesus will come,
    children of God we shall become.
No more pain,
    only eternal life to gain.
But for now hear our praise as a gentle breeze,
    as I walk through this world's leaves
    . . . hoping to please.

This encouraging word is brought to you by

WinePress Publishing from the book,
Batons by **Valerie Klerk**.

To order your copy,
call toll-free 877-421-READ

We Shall Meet Again

Oh, little one . . . time will pass quickly.
You're resting now in a sleep of heavenly peace.
Soon we shall meet again, and what laughter
    will be heard.
I can just imagine the beauty that awaits us.
A wall made out of jasper as far as the eye could see,
    and a city of pure gold, as pure as glass.
Not to mention gates made of pearl.
And when we take our first stroll on those streets of gold,
I wonder of the face I'll behold.
Illuminated by the light of God's glory,
    and fashioned by God's own hand.
It was not His choice for us to care for you
    here on earth.
He wanted you now for reasons of His own,
    not for us to question.
Heart crushed tears from our sudden departing,
    but you have no worry my dear.
Jesus is the lamp that will light our path
    to bring us together for an eternity,
    when we shall meet again.

This encouraging word is brought to you by

WinePress Publishing from the book,
Batons by **Valerie Klerk**.

To order your copy,
call toll-free 877-421-READ

Weep Not for Me

Weep not for me for I have only fallen asleep.
A new day will dawn when the triumph sounds.
In the light of God's glory . . . I'll walk those
    streets of gold.
Laughter and prayer filled my life here on earth.
Guided by God's Holy Spirit and enveloped with
    a family that loved me so.
Many words unspoken as I am laid to rest but
    God knows my heart the best.
Sorrow and grief by a sudden departure.
Weep not for me for I have only fallen asleep.
A new life, a new hope, given to me in a moment
    an in a twinkle of an eye.
Fret not, my Father just wanted me home,
    for reason of His own.
Cherish the moments . . . life on earth.
Only a breath to sing His praise.
Weep not for me . . . for I've gone home.

This encouraging word is brought to you by

WinePress Publishing from the book,
Batons by **Valerie Klerk**.

To order your copy,
call toll-free 877-421-READ

Welcome to My Heart

It is not everyday one peers into another's heart,
    but this day have I chosen for you.
Time passes as the fading flowers of spring.
With the grip of emotions as a gentle breeze,
    let me embrace you with the friendship
    you have so willingly given to me.
Though our time together spent, are not without thorns.
I know a man that wore them well, with
    compassion and with a greater love than I
    could ever imagine to possess.
His love heals the wounds this world inflicts.
    A heart as delicate and frail as a flower
    burst forth with His beauty.
He has allowed it to bloom once again.
May the drops that fall upon this heart be
    as tears of thanks to you alone, oh God,
    for another season with this friend.
With His love and mine . . . my friend,

This encouraging word is brought to you by

WinePress Publishing from the book,
Batons by **Valerie Klerk**.

To order your copy,
call toll-free 877-421-READ

When Souls Collide

When souls collide,
    grace allows them to glide
to a safe haven, sequestered under the
    wings of a merciful God.
A song of praise for His glory raised.
His Holy Spirit a thermal to a soul,
    carrying you to places . . . yet to behold.
What will you say to the souls?
    Would your anger unfold?
Would the light of Christ be darkened by self,
    an abyss of emotion enveloped by the
    cares of this world.
Would you fire shots that wound and kill?
Or would you let His light shine bright.
A heart gripped with compassion,
    eyes with visions of mercy.
Ears that hear what His Holy Spirit
    would have you say.
Would you embrace, with a heart
    full of forgiveness.
Remember His saving grace,
    when souls collide.

This encouraging word is brought to you by

WinePress Publishing from the book,
***Batons* by Valerie Klerk**.

To order your copy,
call toll-free 877-421-READ

Winds of Mercy

If we boast, let us boast in the Lord.
How He works in the soul of man, for in
    our weakness His power is made perfect.
With our hands raised,
    we give our praise.
From glory to glory He leads us
    along our way.
With His hand of mercy stretched out wide,
He leads us across the countryside.
How the world tears at our soul . . .
    and His grace unfolds.
When the gale forces of the world
    want to carry us away.
We cry "Please help us along our way."
A prayer for forgiveness of our sinful ways.
The winds whisper your Word,
    "Be still and know that I am God."
Your Holy Spirit comforts us and leads
    us along our way.
Winds of mercy . . . I thought I heard Him say.

This encouraging word is brought to you by

WinePress Publishing from the book,
Batons by **Valerie Klerk**.

To order your copy,
call toll-free 877-421-READ

Words That Wound

The world clangs and clatters with its chatter
    of words tearing at a soul.
Destruction, despair, chaos, and confusion
    will always be found there.
Tools of the enemy wield at a soul,
    as a sword wielded in battle.
'Tis a fight even in a calm gentle day,
    as children we play.
In a world filled with evil seeking to devour.
For the one who has built their life
    on the rock . . . Jesus Christ.
When the words of the world are wielded,
    they build with skill.
Destruction . . . their hidden sins unfold.
    Thankfulness for . . .
    the mercy of God they behold.
Despair . . . self as scales to blind.
    A song of praise for . . .
    Jesus heals the blind.
Chaos . . . life demands pull from all directions.
    His Holy Spirit consumes your soul . . .
    and in His peace you find correction.
Confusion . . . noise as words that has slashed
    at your soul today.
You hear His Word "Be still and know that I am God,"
    and you find yourself on the narrow way.

So when people's words clang, clatter and wound your soul, remember it's by His stripes we are healed . . . and His grace you'll behold.

This encouraging word is brought to you by

WinePress Publishing from the book,
Batons by **Valerie Klerk**.

To order your copy,
call toll-free 877-421-READ

Song

Have You Ever Seen Me?

Chorus:
Have you ever seen me
    walking in the rain?
Have you ever seen me
    dancing while at play?
Have you ever seen me
    singing along the way?
Oh Lord Jesus do you hear me when I pray?
Oh Lord Jesus can you see this heart dancing a tune for thee?

Our journey is long, but only a breath when you gaze at eternity.
Do you hear the unspoken cries from hearts broken?
The pitter-patter of a child's feet running to talk with you.
Strong and mighty; we stand in awe of you, oh God.

Chorus

We see the gentleness of an awesome God
    as a simple flower blooms.
Overwhelmed by the breath we take
    knowing you alone breathe life into man.
Your mercy and grace framed on a cross.
    A life freely given for a debt I owed.
Have I ever told you, "Thank you"?
    Ah! Our talk this morning you know it touched me so.

Chorus:

The day has started and its time for me to go.
Time slips away. May your praise be sung through the day.
A world full of injustice berates this soul as it labors through the day,
 but your grace is sufficient for me.
Dance I may as you lead from glory to glory.

Chorus:

This encouraging song is brought to you by

WinePress Publishing from the book,
Batons by **Valerie Klerk**.

To order your copy,
call toll-free 877-421-READ

Song

Snow Capped Mountains

Chorus:
Snow capped mountains to a crystal rain
    spring time rivers to a morning summer mist.
Dancing in the leaves of autumn,
    to a winter rest.
A gentle breeze on an ocean floor,
    a new earth you will restore.

One day the clouds will break and from
    heaven you'll take a bride adorned for your Son's sake.
Heaven's gate will open wide to receive His Bride.
    A life covered with sin to be justified within.
The gentle touch of a bee's wings as
    he flutters about, we sing our praise.
The world has no sting to those who
    sing from a pure heart.

Chorus

Your glory shines from the mountain tops,
    Sovereign in all you do.
From the throne of God living waters flow.
    Hear our praise today "What an Awesome God you are!"
"What an Awesome God you are!"

Mighty in all your ways.
A gift given, Christ your Son.
    To Calvary and the cross He wore,
    the price paid, for the sins He bore.

Chorus

Held in the arms of a Merciful God
    caressed by His ever lasting love.
Your word echoes within the heart
    of the soul of man.
Grace covers us like a snow cap on a mountain top.
    Majestic is your Son.
Living water bubbles from a heart,
    music to a melody.
Seasons of life, rivers of trials
    thunders from this world.
Overcomers embraced in your Word.
Dancing in the glory of your praise.
As we are laid to rest.

Chorus

This encouraging song is brought to you by

WinePress Publishing from the book,
Batons by **Valerie Klerk**.

To order your copy,
call toll-free 877-421-READ

To order additional copies of

BATONS

Have your credit card ready and call

Toll free: (877) 421-READ

or send $11.95* each plus $4.95 S&H** to

WinePress Publishing
PO Box 428
Enumclaw, WA 98022

or order online at: www.winepresspub.com

*WA residents, add 8.4% sales tax

**add $1.50 S&H for each additional book ordered